ideals®
THANKSGIVING

Brave and high-souled Pilgrims, you who knew no
   fears,
How your words of thankfulness go ringing down
   the years;
May we follow after; like you, work and pray,
And with hearts of thankfulness keep Thanksgiving
   Day.

Annette Wynne

ISBN 0-8249-1038-9 350

IDEALS — Vol. 42, No. 7 September MCMLXXXV IDEALS (ISSN 0019-137X) is published eight times a year,
February, March, May, June, August, September, November, December
by IDEALS PUBLISHING CORPORATION, Nelson Place at Elm Hill Pike, Nashville, Tenn. 37214
Second class postage paid at Nashville, Tennessee and additional mailing offices.
Copyright © MCMLXXXV by IDEALS PUBLISHING CORPORATION.
POSTMASTER: Send address changes to Ideals, Post Office Box 148000, Nashville, Tenn. 37214
All rights reserved. Title IDEALS registered U.S. Patent Office.
Published simultaneously in Canada.

SINGLE ISSUE — $3.50
ONE YEAR SUBSCRIPTION — eight consecutive issues as published — $15.95
TWO YEAR SUBSCRIPTION — sixteen consecutive issues as published — $27.95
Outside U.S.A., add $4.00 per subscription year for postage and handling

The cover and entire contents of IDEALS are fully protected by copyright and must
not be reproduced in any manner whatsoever. Printed and bound in U.S.A.
by The Banta Co., Menasha, Wisconsin.

Publisher, Patricia A. Pingry
Editor/Ideals, Dorothy L. Gibbs
Managing Editor, Marybeth Owens
Photographic Editor, Gerald Koser
Research Editor, Linda Robinson
Editorial Assistant, Carmen Johnson
Editorial Assistant, Amanda Barrickman
Phototypesetter, Kim Kaczanowski
Art Director, Patrick McRae
Staff Artist, David Lenz

*Front and Back Covers
AUTUMN SCENIC
Waits River, VT
Fred Sieb*

Give Me
A Grateful Heart, Lord

Give me a grateful heart, Lord,
For each small favor granted.
As years unfold, may I behold
Life, still, through eyes enchanted.
Let me find beauty in all things,
Not be too blind to see
The goodness in my fellowman,
That he would find in me.

Grant that my ears remain attuned
To hear the smallest sigh,
And may I lend a gentle touch,
To those less sure than I.
Let me remember lessons learned,
To profit from the past,
And may I build a bridge of dreams,
That shall forever last.

Let me rejoice in simple things;
I need no wealth to buy
The scent of pine upon the wind,
A burnished copper sky,
Scarlet roses on the fence,
Sunrise through the trees —
Oh, grant that I may not outgrow
Affinity for these!

Give me a grateful heart, Lord;
Let me be satisfied
When days are less than sunny
And plans lie at low tide.
Life is a sweet adventure
That will lead to who knows where,
So, give me a grateful heart, Lord,
That I may always care.

Grace E. Easley

Photo Opposite
CRAFTBURY COMMON
Vermont
Fred Sieb

November
Woods

Lovely are the silent woods
  in gray November days,
When the leaves fall red and gold
  about the quiet ways,
From massive beech, majestic oak
  and birches white and slim,
Like the pillared aisles of a cathedral
  vast and dim.

Drifting mist like smoking incense
  hangs upon the air . . .
Along the paths where birds once sang
  the trees stand stripped and bare,
Making Gothic arches
  with their branches interlaced,
And windows framing vistas,
  richly wrought and finely traced.

It is good to be in such a place
  on such a day . . .
Problems vanish from the mind
  and sorrows steal away;
In the woods of gray November
  silent and austere,
Nature gives her benediction
  to the passing year.

Patience Strong

This Is November

Frost on the rooftops,
Dew on the grass,
Leaves drifting down
Wherever we pass;
Wet windy weather,
Skies often gray,
Leaves piling up
Though raked every day.

Ice on the puddles,
Trees almost bare;
Mornings are chilly,
Breath on the air.
Squirrels are still busy,
Where nuts can be found,
Hiding their treasures
In hollows around.

Darkness comes early,
It's cozy indoors
With apples and popcorn
And books to explore.
The harvest is in
And all stored away;
Watch for the snowflakes
To come any day.

Harriet C. Whipple

Song of Thanksgiving

That I was born in this Land of the Free
With its rock-ribbed coast and Redwood tree,
With its maple groves and pines that sing,
Its lakes and rivers and mountains that fling
Their tops in beauty into the sky,
And rolling meadows that boundless lie,
    My thanks I give.

That Freedom is mine in this wonder-land,
To work as I will with mind or hand,
To worship God as I deem it best,
To seek adventure in daring quest;
That my life is mine to build as I will,
My garden, my acres, mine to till,
    My thanks I give.

That America lives, the Home of the Free,
Prairies and orchards from sea to sea;
That mine is the power to help her grow,
To keep her strong, drive out each foe;
For all the blessings my country gives,
Her hopes, her vision that ever lives,
    My thanks I give.

Edna Greene Hines

The Thankful Heart

For all that God in mercy sends —
For health and children, home and friends;
For comforts in the time of need,
For every kindly word or deed,
For happy thoughts and holy talk,
For guidance in our daily walk —
In everything give thanks.

For beauty in this world of ours,
For verdant grass and lovely flowers,
For song of birds, for hum of bees,
For the refreshing Summer breeze,
For hill and plain, for stream and wood,
For the great ocean's mighty flood —
In everything give thanks.

For the sweet sleep which comes with night,
For the returning morning light,
For the bright sun that shines on high,
For the stars glittering in the sky —
For these and everything we see,
O Lord, our hearts we lift to Thee;
In everything give thanks.

Helen Isabella Tupper

The Legend of the Chrysanthemum

There is a timeless quality in the symmetric beauty of November's flower, the chrysanthemum, and the legends surrounding this hardy perennial are as numerous as its fragrant petals. One of the most beautiful of these legends comes from the Orient. It tells of a hermit sage who lived outside a small Oriental village in the fourteenth century.

For many years, the people of the village had been guided by the hermit's wisdom and advice. One winter, when a group of villagers came to see the sage, they discovered that he had gone, but had left for them a bowl of seeds with a note which read, "Wisdom is a glorious thing, perfection a joy to behold." The villagers did not understand the reason of the hermit's words. Nevertheless, they took the seeds back to the village and planted them the following spring.

The old sage was never seen again, but, in the fall, hundreds of bright flowers sprang up from the seeds he had left behind. The petals of the flowers were as numerous as the hermit's bits of wisdom, and their symmetry made them the picture of perfection. It was then that the villagers realized the meaning of the hermit's message. They came to cherish the brilliant flowers for their beauty, just as they had revered the sage for his wisdom.

The chrysanthemum was later named the flower of the Orient. In the language of flowers, it is the symbol of perfection and long life.

Carl Goeller

Photo Opposite
GOLDEN CHRYSANTHEMUMS
Fred Sieb

Mamie Ozburn Odum

Newton County, Georgia, the only county in the state with an officially appointed poet laureate, chose Mamie Ozburn Odum for the honor in 1945. She held the title for thirty years, until her death in 1975. Although she wrote stories, articles, and essays as well as poems, she said her poetry came first. "It seems as if I was cut out to write poetry. Even when I was little, my mother would get exasperated with me for rhyming everything I said." Over the years Mrs. Odum won many awards, both national and international, for her poems.

She was a woman of other talents as well. She crocheted dozens of afghans, making sure that there was one for each child, grandchild, and great-grandchild. She played a variety of musical instruments — the banjo, the harmonica, the guitar, an old-fashioned harp, and, what may have been her favorite, the organ. At one time she had a collection of nine organs! Mrs. Odum also taught Sunday school for fifty years.

Outside her rambling, Victorian home in Covington, Georgia, she kept an acre of land for a garden. There she grew over 300 varieties of day lilies and sixty different types of camellias. Next to her family and her poems, her garden was her greatest joy.

When asked for her philosophy of life, she had two replies: "Count that day lost when at setting sun, no worthwhile deed has been done." And, "I never trouble trouble till trouble troubles me — and *then* I don't let it bother anybody else."

The Thankful Season

As springtime turns to summer,
So does gay autumn call,
And hearts fill with Thanksgiving
When we greet cool days of fall.

When summer turns to autumn,
The harvest days are sweet,
The apple trees are laden
With luscious fruits to eat.

The yams are hilled and ready
For winter-time supplies,
Bright orange pumpkins wait
To make our golden pumpkin pies.

We bring in seasoned firewood
To make a cozy blaze,
And we dream of spending Winter
In quiet, homey ways.

Gifts

Give thanks for every sunset,
For flowers on the hill,
For silver moonlight overhead,
For songs of whippoorwills.

Give thanks for friends and neighbors,
For the laughter of a child,
For family life and hearthstones,
For weather, brisk or mild.

Give thanks for all gifts given,
For home and family ties,
For mother's love and father's care,
For leaders strong and wise.

Give heartfelt thanks — be grateful
For all that you possess,
And when, each year, you gather
Give thanks you've been so blessed.

Some Small Gift

I pray each day for some small gift,
Some simple thing to fill my soul,
A cloud with flecks of gold and blue,
A bird's sweet anthem from the knoll,
A coral vine upon a wall,
A soothing, singing, long-leaf pine,
Some hickory nuts from the pasture lane,
Some scuppernongs like purple wine.

I pray each day for some small gift,
Yet, knowing life, there must be pain,
But daily gifts of little things
Are like the sunshine after rain.
Grant me wisdom to do right,
Give honest work for honest pay,
And, 'fore I fall asleep each night,
Give thanks for gifts received each day.

Thanksgiving

Thank You, Lord, for deep green hills,
Homes with laughter, love, and song,
And bread that comes by sweat of brow,
New strength to work the whole day long.
Knowing Thee, we praise in prayer,
Safe and warm from winter's cold;
Give us peace of mind and soul,
Instill new love as we grow old.
Vanquish our selfish hearts and plans,
Inspire us to be forgiving
Now, and may we be content
Giving thanks for each Thanksgiving.

Autumn Glory

While walking in the woods today,
I marvelled at the bright array
Of Autumn robes the trees had donned.
How blue the tranquil sky beyond!
Could this be real — this fairyland
Of red and gold? And there I'd stand
Enraptured, far as eye could see,
At Mother Nature's artistry.

The maples wore rich, gold brocade;
The oaks wore red, the balsams jade;
The stately elms in jasmine dressed,
As did the willows; And the rest
Were garbed in splendor, one and all,
For their majestic Harvest Ball.
And, underneath, in their cool shade,
Wild asters, ferns and gentians played.

Helen D. Hering

Photo Opposite
AUTUMN REFLECTIONS
Fred Sieb

Nutty Snacks

Pecan Pie Bars
Makes 32 bars

2 cups flour
1 cup packed brown sugar
½ cup butter
½ cup margarine
5 eggs

1 cup dark corn syrup
¾ cup granulated sugar
Dash salt
1 teaspoon vanilla
1 cup broken pecans

Preheat oven to 350°. In a large mixing bowl, combine flour and brown sugar. Cut in butter and margarine with a pastry blender or two knives until mixture resembles coarse crumbs. Press crumb mixture into a 9 x 13-inch baking pan. Bake for 10 minutes or until golden. While crust is baking, combine eggs, corn syrup, granulated sugar, salt, and vanilla; blend well. Stir in pecans. Pour filling over hot crust; reduce oven temperature to 275° and bake for 50 minutes or until center is set. Cool in pan on a wire rack before cutting into bars.

Almond Popcorn Crunch
Makes approximately 3 quarts

2 cups granulated sugar
1 cup light brown sugar
¾ cup light corn syrup
1¼ cups water

1 tablespoon salt
2½ cups whole *or* coarsely chopped almonds
½ cup butter, softened
3 quarts popped popcorn

In an 5-quart saucepan, combine sugars, corn syrup, water, and salt; cook to 235° on a candy thermometer. Add almonds; cook to 250°, stirring occasionally. Continue cooking to 295°, stirring constantly. Add butter; stir until melted and completely blended into the syrup mixture. Remove mixture from heat; add half of the popcorn. Stir syrup up from the bottom of the pan, coating corn well. Pour remaining popcorn into a large buttered bowl. Pour syrup mixture over the popcorn in the bowl; stir until all corn is covered and almonds are distributed evenly. Spread mixture onto a cold, buttered surface; break apart with two forks.

Fruit and Nut Nibble
Makes 10 cups

½ cup sugar
½ teaspoon cinnamon
¼ teaspoon nutmeg
¼ teaspoon ground cloves
¼ teaspoon ground ginger
2 cups pecans
2 cups whole almonds

2 cups cashews
1 quart vegetable oil
Salt
2 cups carob-covered peanuts
1 cup dried apricots, cut in half
1 cup raisins

In a small bowl, combine sugar and spices; set aside. In a large saucepan, mix nuts together. Add water to cover nuts; bring to a boil. Boil for 1 minute. Drain nuts well; pat with paper towels to remove excess moisture. While nuts are still warm, toss with the sugar mixture. Spread sugared nuts onto a tray in a single layer; let dry for 8 to 24 hours. In a large saucepan or deep fryer, heat oil to 350°. Fry nuts in small batches for 2 minutes or until sugar caramelizes and nuts are dark brown. Drain well and cool; sprinkle with salt. Add peanuts, apricots, and raisins; mix well. Store mixture in an airtight container.

A Thought

It is very nice to think
The world is full of meat and drink,
With little children saying grace
In every Christian kind of place.

Robert Louis Stevenson

A Child's Grace

Some hae meat and canna eat,
And some wad eat that want it;
But we hae meat and we can eat,
And sae the Lord be thankit.

Robert Burns

All in a Word

T for time to be together,
  turkey, talk, and tangy weather.

H for harvest stored away,
  home, and hearth, and holiday.

A for autumn's frosty art,
  and abundance in the heart.

N for neighbors, and November,
  nice-things, new-things to remember.

K for kitchen, kettles croon —
  with kith and kin expected soon.

S for sizzles, sights, and sounds,
  and something-special that abounds.

That spells THANKS ... for joy of living
  and a jolly good Thanksgiving.

Aileen Fisher

Something to Be Thankful For

I'm glad that I am not to-day
A chicken or a goose,
Or any other sort of bird
That is of any use.

I rather be a little girl,
Although 'tis very true,
The things I do not like at all,
I'm often made to do.

I rather eat some turkey than
To be one, thick and fat,
And so, with all my heart, to-day,
I'll thankful be for that.

Clara J. Denton

Thank You, God

Thank you, God, for loving care;
Thank you for the clothes we wear.
Thank you for our homes and food;
You are always kind and good.

Thank you for our strength and health,
For our country's harvest wealth.
Thank you for love, life, and joy.
Thanks from every girl and boy.

Unknown

A Thanksgiving Memory

When Mom would baste the turkey,
We kids could hardly wait!
The smell of all that cooking,
The pies upon the plate,
The cranberries, red and juicy,
The dressing, golden-brown,
Potatoes, mashed and ready —
Can't we, please, sit down?

When Mom would baste the turkey,
We knew she soon would say,
"Come! Count your many blessings
On this Thanksgiving Day."
We'd all hold hands together
And bow our heads in prayer.
It was a happy moment
With all our loved ones there.

When Mom would baste the turkey,
My heart would glow with love!
Our home, so warm and peaceful,
Was blessed by heaven above.
Mom made our gatherings special
In a warm and loving way,
And I'll always have her near me
On each Thanksgiving Day.

Nelle Hardgrove

We Thank Thee

We thank Thee, Lord, for pumpkin pie
And turkey with its filling,
For sweet potatoes, cranberries,
And appetites so willing!

We thank Thee, Lord, for laughter,
A savory spice for any meal,
For love and fellowship and faith
That fills our lives with zeal!

We thank Thee, Lord, for families
Who gather far and near!
For sister, brother, father, mother
And all we hold most dear!

We thank Thee for the many blessings
That touch our lives each day,
We pray we'll bless the lives we touch
As we travel down life's way!

Kay Hoffman

Overleaf
AUTUMN VILLAGE
East Topsham, VT
Bob Clemenz

A Thanksgiving Dinner Question

Pumpkin or mince, which will it be?
That's a favorite Thanksgiving question for me.
Pumpkin is sweet and spicy, it's true,
But mince is tangy, and seasonal, too.

Pumpkin has whipped cream, a most luscious treat,
But mince has its rum sauce, so smooth and so sweet.
I ponder, debate, but it's always the same;
I just can't decide which pie I should name.

Pumpkin or mince, which will it be?
"A little of both!" is the answer from me.

Craig E. Sathoff

Hurrah! For the Pumpkin Pie

What Thanksgiving dinner would be complete without a delicious, generous serving of rich pumpkin pie? Most Americans would be quick to agree that the celebration would be lacking without it. Yet, how many of them really understand their sentiment for this orange-colored purée in a simple flour and water crust. We have to look back to find the reasoning behind our "pumpkin love," for it is as old as the New World.

The Indians of North America had long used pumpkins and other types of squash. The sturdy shells made good containers. Dried gourds served as ceremonial rattles. Squash and pumpkin seeds were edible and could be pressed to extract their exotic oils. Pumpkin meat could be boiled for soup or dried and ground into meal for use in breads and puddings. The settlers of New England adopted the Indians' bright orange vegetable, and it quickly became an indispensable part of their diet.

Highly nutritious and capable of being stored throughout the winter, the pumpkin provided hearty eating for a hard-working and hungry settlement. New World housewives would dice ripe pumpkins and stew them over a low fire; butter, vinegar, and ginger often were added to enhance the pumpkin's sweet flavor. The stewed pumpkin was then used in a number of ways, as this old colonial verse humorously documents:

> For pottage and puddings, and custards, and pies,
> Our pumpkins and parsnips are common supplies.
> We have pumpkins at morning and pumpkins at noon;
> If it were not for pumpkins, we should be undoon.

Pumpkin pie in early New England was quite different from our modern version. It was made by slicing off the top of the pumpkin, removing the seeds, and filling the cavity with milk, spices, and a natural sweetener, such as maple syrup. Then, the whole thing was baked!

As Thanksgiving became a yearly event, pumpkin pie grew in popularity. It became so important, in fact, that, in 1705, Colchester, Connecticut actually postponed Thanksgiving until their supply of molasses arrived. The pumpkin pies could not be made without it!

Pumpkin pie has remained significant to this day. The poet Whittier encapsulated "pumpkin love" so eloquently when he asked:

> What moistens the lip and what brightens the eye?
> What calls back the past, like the rich Pumpkin Pie?

Today we can't imagine Thanksgiving without it. For, indeed, a dinner is just a dinner until you've added the pumpkin pie, the tradition, the real flavor of Thanksgiving.

Cornell M. Brellenthin

From

A Song of Harvest

O Painter of the fruits and flowers!
We thank Thee for thy wise design
Whereby these human hands of ours
In Nature's garden work with Thine.

And thanks that from our daily need
The joy of simple faith is born;
That he who smites the summer weed,
May trust Thee for the autumn corn.

Give fools their gold, and knaves their
    power;
Let fortune's bubbles rise and fall;
Who sows a field, or trains a flower,
Or plants a tree, is more than all.

For he who blesses most is blest;
And God and man shall own his
    worth
Who toils to leave as his bequest
An added beauty to the earth.

And, soon or late, to all that sow,
The time of harvest shall be given;
The flower shall bloom,
    the fruit shall grow,
If not on earth, at last in heaven.

John Greenleaf Whittier

The Day
the Geese
Landed

Many special blessings slip into the life of a farm wife, bringing with them a special feeling of closeness to the Creator. Whenever I'm out in the open fields, I sense a special relationship with God, our landlord. In this relationship, we have never really lacked any of the necessities of life. We've had some lean, hard years of farming, but we've had bountiful ones, too. Yet, sometimes, we have forgotten our blessings. I was keenly reminded of God's holy presence the day the geese landed.

It was a very ordinary, Indian Summer day on the farm. The morning chill crept into my bones, but, by afternoon, it was another beautiful autumn day. I was helping my husband in the field, discing ahead of his tractor as he plowed the stubble underground for the winter. As our tractors wove back and forth across the field, I meditated, a regular custom with me. Then, raising my eyes to the beautiful skies, I gasped at what I saw.

In a shower of fluttering wings, hundreds of blue and Canadian snow geese settled down to rest and feed in the field I was discing. While I always watch the spring and fall skies for these majestic birds, this was the first time I had ever seen them so close. Their heads bobbed on long, graceful necks as they gleaned left-over grain from the field. A noisy chorus, that could be heard above the roar of my tractor, kept them in touch with each other as they ate.

I will never forget the awe I felt as I disced back and forth, not fifty feet from them. For over two hours they fed and rested, all the while watching me as I worked. Each time I made a round, they carefully kept their distance from my machine, never flying, but moving a bit farther away where they felt safer.

On my final run across the field, I throttled the tractor down so I could hear their noisy chit-chat better, but a single backfire from the engine ended their visit in a hurry. With the mighty whirr of a thousand wings, they soared off into the heavens, lost against a beautiful sunset.

How can anyone who lives with nature and works with the soil take such beautiful moments for granted? They are special blessings with, perhaps, a message from God: To all things there is a season; a time to heed the heavenly plan. It is no accident that the geese know just when and where to go each year, and it is a blessing to enjoy. I know that I will never forget the feeling in my heart the day the geese landed.

Iris Hanson

It is good to give thanks to the Lord,

to sing praises to thy name O Most High;

to declare thy steadfast love in the morning,

and thy faithfulness by night,

to the music of the lute and the harp,

to the melody of the lyre.

For thou, O Lord, hast made me glad by thy work;

at the works of thy hands I sing for joy.

Psalm 92:1-4

Atlantic Charter,
A. D. 1620-1942

What are you carrying Pilgrims, Pilgrims?
What did you carry beyond the sea?
  We carried the Book, we carried the Sword,
  A steadfast heart in the fear of the Lord,
  And a living faith in His plighted word
  That all men should be free.

What were your memories, Pilgrims, Pilgrims?
What of the dreams you bore away?
  We carried the songs our fathers sung
  By the hearths of home when they were young,
  And the comely words of the mother-tongue
  In which they learnt to pray.

What did you find there, Pilgrims, Pilgrims?
What did you find beyond the waves?
   A stubborn land and a barren shore,
   Hunger and want and sickness sore:
   All these we found and gladly bore
   Rather than be slaves.

How did you fare there, Pilgrims? Pilgrims?
What did you build in that stubborn land?
   We felled the forest and tilled the sod
   Of a continent no man had trod
   And we established there, in the Grace of God,
   The rights whereby we stand.

What are you bringing us, Pilgrims, Pilgrims?
Bringing us back in this bitter day?
   The selfsame things we carried away:
   The Book, the Sword,
   The fear of the Lord,
   And the boons our fathers dearly bought:
   Freedom of Worship, Speech and Thought,
   Freedom from Want, Freedom from Fear,
   The liberties we hold most dear,
   And who shall say us Nay?

Francis Brett Young

"Atlantic Charter" from THE ISLAND by Francis Brett Young, copyright 1942 by Francis Brett Young, published by Farrar, Straus, & Co., Inc. Reprinted by permission of Watkins/Loomis Agency, Inc.

Overleaf
JAMES FORT
Jamestown, VA
H. Armstrong Roberts

Squanto Plants the Corn

When the young Sky Woman fell,
   flung from her celestial lodge
   by the irate Chief of Heaven
   in a mystifying rage,
   she carried with her five good gifts —
   tobacco, beans, squash, fish, and corn —
   and became the Great Earth Mother,
   nurturing all forms of life.

   So musing, Squanto kneeled down,
      red kernels in his own red hand,
      motioning the tall white men
      beside him to bend down and watch,
      for Earth Mother had borne all men,
      so these were brothers at his side,
      and maize was theirs, as well as his,
      although they did not seem to know
      how to place it in the earth
      in a small five-kerneled mound,
      (in memory of the five good gifts,)
      with a fish to fertilize —

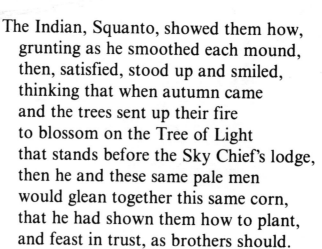

      The Indian, Squanto, showed them how,
         grunting as he smoothed each mound,
         then, satisfied, stood up and smiled,
         thinking that when autumn came
         and the trees sent up their fire
         to blossom on the Tree of Light
         that stands before the Sky Chief's lodge,
         then he and these same pale men
         would glean together this same corn,
         that he had shown them how to plant,
         and feast in trust, as brothers should.

Gloria Maxson

Feast of Friendship

The tall Indian rose before the sun. In the chill December air, he wrapped his deerskin robe around his broad shoulders and watched the faint, pale fingers of dawn reaching up the eastern sky. In the distance, seagulls swooped over the low fog that hugged the Atlantic coastline. Their eerie calls echoed in the damp forest.

For the past three days, the Indian, Chief Massasoit, and ninety of his braves had been guests of the Pilgrim settlers. Now, on his final morning at Plymouth, he stepped silently over the other sleeping Indians and went to stand on the wooded rise above the settlement. Thin wisps of smoke from seven large chimneys hovered over the seven tiny houses below. In these small lodgings dwelt fifty souls — strangers to him just a year ago. Massasoit allowed his mind to wander, to drift with the morning mist, settling here and there on a memory.

These were the first white men and women he had come to know well, and something in their collective spirit appealed to him. It was not because of their abilities, he thought; they were not good hunters or fishers, nor were they expert builders. Their farming skills, too, were sadly lacking. But they had endured much during their first year in his country, and they had survived.

Massasoit recalled how the Pilgrims had been so cruelly tested. They built — and watched their first structure go down in flames. They planted — and saw their first crops come up shriveled and small. Yet, they plodded on. Bitter winter storms and starvation cut their numbers in half. Children were orphaned; babes died

Photo Above, PILGRIM WIFE, Plimoth Plantation, Fred Dole

Photo Above, PILGRIM, Plimoth Plantation, Fred Dole

in their mothers' arms. Yet, the survivors endured with courage, praying daily to their God and drawing ever closer to one another. The Wampanoag chief admired their tenacity, their strong determination, and their calm, quiet faith in the God they served.

When, after the final autumn harvest, the Pilgrims invited him to share their Feast of Thanks, he was most anxious to attend. Now the chief smiled broadly remembering his arrival at the settlement three days ago.

Although he had been greeted with honor and respect, Massasoit sensed the Pilgrims' shocked surprise when he entered their outpost with ninety braves, outnumbering the Pilgrims two to one! His hosts seemed even more astonished when the braves, who were used to Indian festivals which lasted several days, began to make camp. Nevertheless, hospitality reigned, and the planned feast did indeed become a festival. Bountiful meals were graciously prepared, although there were only five women in the settlement to make them. Roasted game and fish, baked eels and clams, savory chowders, soups, and stews were still a vivid memory. Feeding one hundred forty hungry souls, however, had severely depleted the settlement's supplies. Realizing this, Massasoit sent his hunters to the forest. They returned with five large deer to replenish the dwindling stores.

The days of feasting passed quickly, full of contests and challenges. William Bradford, governor of the settlement, marched his troops in formation and had them demonstrate for the Indians a dramatic contrast of exploding muskets and blaring bugles. Massasoit, in turn, had his braves entertain the Pilgrims with samples of Indian prowess with bow and arrow. They shared stories, skills, and songs, blending their individual melodies into a unique harmony of sound and spirit.

As the sun brightened the December sky, the tall chief returned from his reverie knowing that much more than a feast had been shared in that outpost below him. He knew, also, that those brave men and women, who had faced fear and famine, death and discouragement to carve out a new beginning in his country, were worthy of the land they had claimed between the forest and the sea. They were worthy, too, of his friendship — and so he would pledge.

Pamela Kennedy

A New England Thanksgiving

The following is from an account of Thanksgiving dinner written in 1779 by Juliana Smith of Massachusetts in a letter to her cousin, Betsey. Juliana copied the letter into her diary, a common practice of the times so that carefully written letters would not be lost in transmission. Juliana's diary was discovered by one of her descendants, Helen Evertson Smith, who allowed the material to be published.

This year it was Uncle Simeon's turn to have the dinner at his house, but of course we all helped them as they help us when it is our turn, & there is always enough for us all to do. All the baking of pies & cakes was done at our house & we had the big oven heated & filled twice each day for three days before it was all done, & *everything was* GOOD, though we did have to do without some things that ought to be used. Neither Love nor Money could buy Raisins, but our good red cherries dried without the pits, did

almost as well & happily Uncle Simeon still had some spices in store....

"Our Mince Pies were good although we had to use dried Cherries as I told you, & the meat was shoulder of Venisson, instead of Beef. The Pumpkin Pies, Apple Tarts & big Indian Puddings lacked for nothing save *appetite* by the time we had got round to them....

"There was no Plumb Pudding, but a boiled Suet Pudding, stirred thick with dried Plumbs & Cherries, was called by the old Name & answered the purpose. All the other spice had been used in the Mince Pies, so for this Pudding we used a jar of West India preserved Ginger which chanced to be left of the last shipment which Uncle Simeon had from there, we chopped the Ginger small and stirred it through with the Plumbs and Cherries. It was *extraordinary* goods. The Day was bitter cold & when we got home from Meeting, which Father did not keep over long by reason of the cold, we were glad eno' of the fire in Uncle's Dining Hall, but by the time the dinner was one-half over those of us who were on the fire side of one Table was forced to get up & carry our plates with us around to the far side of the other Table, while those who had sat there were as glad to bring their plates around to the fire side to get warm. All but the Old Ladies who had a screen put behind their chairs.

"Uncle Simeon was in his best mood, and you know how good that is! He kept both Tables in a roar of laughter with his droll stories of the days when he was studying medicine in Edinborough, & afterwards he & Father & Uncle Paul joined in singing Hymns & Ballads. You know how fine their voices go together. Then we all sang a Hymn and afterwards my dear Father led us in prayer, remembering all Absent Friends before the Throne of Grace, & much I wished that my dear Betsey was here as one of us, as she has been of yore.

"We did not rise from the Table until it was quite dark, & then when the dishes had been cleared away we all got round the fire as close as we could, & cracked nuts, & sang songs & told stories. At least some told & others listened. *You know nobody* can exceed the two Grandmothers at telling tales of all the things they have seen themselves, & repeating those of the early years in New England, & even some in the Old England, which they had heard in their youth from their Elders. My Father says it is a goodly custom to hand down all worthy deeds & traditions from Father to Son, as the Israelites were commanded to do about Passover & as the Indians here have always done, because the Word that is spoken is remembered longer than the one that is written . . . ."

Helen Evertson Smith

Franklin's Choice

Had Benjamin Franklin had his way, there would be no "American" eagle. Rather, we would have a wild turkey as the emblem of our country. Here, taken from a letter to his daughter, Sarah Bache, on January 26, 1784, is Franklin's own account of his feelings about our national bird.

For my own part, I wish the Bald Eagle had not been chosen as the Representative of our Country; he is a Bird of bad moral Character; he does not get his living honestly; you may have seen him perch'd on some dead Tree, near the River where, too lazy to fish for himself, he watches the Labour of the Fishing-Hawk; and, when that diligent Bird has at length taken a Fish, and is bearing it to his Nest for the support of his Mate and young ones, the Bald Eagle pursues him, and takes it from him. With all this Injustice he is never in good Case; but, like those among Men who live by Sharping and Robbing, he is generally poor, and often very lousy. Besides, he is a rank Coward; the little King Bird, not bigger than a sparrow, attacks him boldly and drives him out of the District....

I am, on this account, not displeas'd that the Figure is not known as a Bald Eagle, but looks more like a Turk'y. For in Truth, the Turk'y is in comparison a much more respectable Bird, and withal a true original Native of America. Eagles have been found in all Countries, but the Turk'y was peculiar to ours; the first of the Species seen in Europe being brought to France by the Jesuits from Canada, and serv'd up at the Wedding Table of Charles the Ninth. He is, though a little vain and silly, it is true, but not the worse emblem for that, a Bird of Courage, and would not hesitate to attack a Grenadier of the British Guards, who should presume to invade his Farm Yard with a red Coat on.

. . . the Turk'y is . . . a much more respectable Bird,
and withal a true original Native of America.

Readers' Reflections

Autumn

Autumn sees the leaves dance
And flaunt their colors bold.
A gilt-edged, lovely, falling time,
It turns the earth to gold.

Autumn ends the harvest
And breathes old thanks-filled tunes.
A fruitful, swollen, storing time,
It hangs huge, yellow moons.

Autumn dresses morning
In a muted gray-fog coat.
A ghostly, muffled, sleeping time,
It whispers silvered notes.

Autumn guides the waterfowl
Down old ancestral ways.
A peaceful, far-voiced, flying time,
It heralds winter days.

Mike Logan
Helena, Montana

Happy Thanksgiving

We've got to catch the turkey
(He's out behind the gate)
And find the nicest pumpkin
Before it is too late.

The cookie jar is brimming;
The cakes are almost done.
The candy dish is being filled —
Let's try to sneak just one.

The cranberries are sorted;
I smell some homemade bread,
And Grandma's made some jellies —
My favorite's cherry red.

Soon, when dinner's ready,
We'll all take time to say,
"Thank you, Lord, for all your gifts
On this Thanksgiving Day."

Roselyn Eckel
Long Prairie, Minnesota

Timekeepers

Mama scrapes the last apple butter
from the bottom of a mason jar
she sealed in the early days of May,
and gives it to Papa on warm, brown toast.

Papa sits in front of the late-November fire
blazing bright with the wood
he chopped in June.

Zann Easterwood
Martin, Tennessee

Thanksgiving

Uncles, aunts, and cousins,
Children by the score;
Pots and pans and casseroles,
Recipes galore;

Family members gathered
With happiness to share;
Someone telling tall tales,
Laughter everywhere;

A cozy fire to warm us,
Pumpkins picked for pie;
Neighbors and acquaintances
And friends just dropping by —

Today, we're celebrating
The bounty of the earth.
We're grateful for our blessings,
For life and all its worth.

Sherry Clark Long
Portland, Oregon

Autumn Harvest

This morning I walked out
to drink my coffee with the sun.

Down the path,
I gathered leaves — one red, one gold —
and brought them back to show
to a gray squirrel that wouldn't look,
but dropped acorns through the branches,
then ran away — from tree to tree
and up the hill — until I couldn't see.
Maybe he just got where he was going.

The leaves beside my cup are still —
to touch, to hold.
Here.
One is red,
and one is gold.

Robert C. Jones
Warrensburg, Missouri

Editor's Note: Readers are invited to submit poetry, short anecdotes, and humorous reflections on life for possible publication in future *Ideals* issues. Please send xeroxed copies only; manuscripts will not be returned. Writers will receive $10 for each published submission. Send material to "Readers' Reflections," P.O. Box 1101, Milwaukee, Wisconsin 53201.

JUST A SPRIG...

'Twas just a sprig of bittersweet
I picked along the way,
And yet I took more home with me
Than twig for fall bouquet;

For in each berry there was stored
A spark of summer sun
To brighten up the darkened rooms
At home, when day is done.

June Masters Bacher

OF BITTERSWEET

Bittersweet, climbing or trailing along,
Grows in the woodland and ripens in fall,
Bearing orange berries and oval-shaped leaves,
Anxious to scatter its red-coated seeds.

These seeds will nestle in soft, forest loam,
Finding a rooting place, calling it home.
So in the forest (and life?) it is clear,
There will be a bittersweet, year after year.

Amanda Barrickman

Country Chronicle

Some of the most fulfilling hours of a farm year come at Thanksgiving time, when the crops are in from gardens and fields and the apples have been harvested from the hillside orchards. By then the bluebirds have issued their warbling farewells from the gnarled boughs; the deer have come down from the woods to feed on apples fallen in the grass, and the leaves have been pulled from the trees by the frost and the rain and the wind.

Fall plowing is done. Furrow after furrow of freshly turned loam glistens in the fading light of the November sun. The furrows span the slopes, reaching from fencerow to fencerow and from roadside to brushland thicket. For days in the brilliant glow of October, the plowman kept at his task wanting to finish the work before a hard freeze sealed the soil. As he guided his team across the land, he watched the trees on the hillside being transformed into a canopy of red and gold.

As his reward, barn and farmhouse cellar alike now yield the rich aromas of the ripened year. The mows are filled with timothy and clover brought in from the meadows of summer. Golden ears of husked corn lie in a pile on the smooth, worn planks of the barn floor. The grain bins overflow with oats, barley, and wheat.

Lining the walls of the farmhouse cellar are barrels of apples: the Snows and Baldwins, the Greenings and Northern Spies. There are piles of cabbages, pumpkins, and squash; bins of potatoes; crates of onions; kegs of beets, carrots, and sweet, succulent parsnips. There are canned vegetables, as well as pickles and relishes, cans of berries and fruits, and jars of jellies, jams, and preserves. All are part of the household's stores for the long, slow hours of winter, and all are symbolic of the richness of the soil.

Thanksgiving Day is the ideal time to express our gratitude for the goodness of the land which nurtures and sustains us. Late November, indeed, is appropriate for the festive observance. The curtains of the ebbing season are closing tightly against the nights of ice and snow. Soon the hills will be blanketed with white and a farm stream will murmur softly under its shield of ice, humming a fitting recessional for the waning year.

Lansing Christman

Harvest Time

I often seek the beauty,
Found upon my pantry shelf,
In jars of jams and jellies
I've put up by myself.

There are many splendid colors:
The corn and pickled beets,
The peas and beans and carrots
And other harvest treats.

The fruits of all my labors
Are lined up along the wall.
The applesauce and berries
And peaches for the fall

Say to my loving family
That I have done my best
In putting up the bounty
With which we have been blessed.

The crocks of applebutter
And churns of pickled beans,
The bins of new potatoes,
And hams hung from the beams,

Dried apples, beans, and pumpkins,
Fragrant herbs and teas,
Remind me that my efforts
Will serve my family's needs.

The joy I find in viewing
The fruits from off the vine
Rewards my tired body
At the close of harvesttime.

Sylvia C. Mintz

Photo Opposite
COUNTRY CANNING
Gerald Koser

Old Country Kitchen

The moment that you went inside
Some fragrance came to greet you there —
New applesauce with cinnamon,
The scent of fresh bread on the air;

Johnnycake or gingerbread,
Mincemeat's simmering spicy smell,
And, from the cellar's fragrant bins,
Apple-breath in dark stairwell;

Checkerberry, balsam, mint,
Baking beans in earthen pot,
Molasses candy, lavender,
Sadironed linens sweetly hot;

Hint of sage or caraway,
A potluck supper's savory steam,
Corn popping over glowing coals,
And birchwood smell, sweet as a dream.

Ruth B. Field

Autumn Bonfires

When the briskly blowing breezes
  Send the leaves in showers down,
When they swirl around the tree trunks,
  Come to rest in heaps of brown:
    Then the children in their mirth,
    Tramp them down upon the earth.

Shouts of merry laughter ringing,
  From the throngs of boys and girls
Holding arms to catch the leaflets
  That the wind from tree-tops whirls:
    Then, like some most solemn rite,
    Countless fires they stoop to light.

With the blue smoke upward curling,
  Fragrant with the breath of Fall,
Joining hands they march around them,
  Brightness glinting over all.
    Festive lights the bonfires shed
    As the leaves are put to bed.

Leaping flames are lower falling
  As the gay procession slows;
Filmy smoke makes fairy patterns
  As in ruddiness it glows.
    In the magic, mystic light,
    Wave the leaves the long good-night.

Hazel Adell Jackson

The Ripened Leaves

Said the leaves upon the branches
   One sunny autumn day:
"We've finished all our work, and now
   We can no longer stay.
So our gowns of red and yellow
   And our cloaks of sober brown
Must be worn before the frost comes,
   And we go rustling down.

"We've had a jolly summer
   With the birds that built their nests
Beneath our green umbrellas,
   And the squirrels that were our guests.
But we cannot wait for winter,
   And we do not care for snow;
When we hear the wild northwesters
   We loose our clasp and go.

"But we hold our heads up bravely
   Unto the very last,
And shine in pomp and splendor
   As away we flutter fast.
In the mellow autumn noontide
   We kiss and say goodbye,
And through the naked branches
   Then may children see the sky."

Margaret E. Sangster

A Time Called Autumn

Now, in the time of Autumn,
When the harvest days are past,
When the scarlet leaf grows crisper
And the golden hours can't last,

There comes a time for sleeping
That the earth may have its rest,
For God so rules the seasons
To do what each knows best.

Soon winter will be coming,
And, when the time is right,
God will bed the weary traveler
With coverlet of white.

And, in that winter's sleeping,
What dreams live 'neath the snow?
One sunlit day next April
The grass will let us know.

Minnie Klemme

Photo Opposite
FROSTED LEAVES
Ed Cooper Photo

Warming
the Heart
of America

"Sara, it's here! Go get your brother and sister." Peeping through the snow-frosted panes of the living room windows, the mother's eyes danced with anticipation as she watched her husband and oldest son struggle to unload the 300-pound weight from the bed of their brand-new, green pick-up truck. Within seconds she was joined at the window by two more rapt and curious youngsters. They watched the man and boy jockey the heavyweight onto a rented piano dolly, strap it down, and slowly, ever so carefully, roll the unwieldy cargo up the temporary ramp that spanned the front steps, across the porch, and into the living room.

The children stared, fascinated, as their father and brother gently lowered the treasure, a big, old-fashioned parlor stove, into its place of honor in the corner of the room. Like the staunch Victorian matron that it was, the stove immediately assumed command of the room and all therein. Five feet tall, clothed in impeccable black, wearing a glittering collar and an even more imposing crown, it was a dowager of unquestioned substance.

"It's beautiful!" one child whispered in awe. "Even prettier than in the store."

If you can remember Ty Cobb at bat, or Woodrow Wilson as president, or the sinking of the Titanic, you might have just such a nostalgic scene in your own memory. The arrival of a new parlor stove was, a few generations ago, a moment of exultant pride for any American family.

The gentle warmth of an old potbelly stove can be decidedly more comfortable on a frigid day than gas or electric heat, and a lot more satisfying to cozy up to than a furnace register. Of course, the whole thing is probably psychological. Just seeing fire makes one feel warm, but, as a college professor once mused, "perusing the spring seed catalogs is a lot more fun when you're toasting your toes on the footrest of a friendly little potbellied stove."

Although the early Pilgrim settlers knew the pleasure of toasting toes at an iron stove, it took the genius of Benjamin Franklin, sparked by a firewood shortage around Philadelphia in the early 1740's, to come up with the first really original American contribution to home heating, the "Pennsylvania Fireplace."

Franklin's iron, open-hearth stove was designed to be set into the existing opening of a fireplace and to use the chimney's flue. Since it was smaller than the original fireplace, it used less wood or coal; more smoke went up the chimney than into the room, and more heat went into the room than up the chimney. Another of Mr. Franklin's inventions had become a part of American heritage.

Finding an authentic Pennsylvania Fireplace today is pretty unlikely, but many charming little potbellied stoves have followed in the footsteps of the Franklin. Furthermore, they made stoves in the shape of Swiss chalets and full-maned lions, stoves with intricate grape arbors draped around the firebox, and stoves that resembled nothing in the world so much as Lilliputian Parthenons, complete with fluted columns and overhanging cornices.

We're very fortunate, we Americans; so much about our roots still lies within the memories of so many. The old iron stoves are part of those roots. They are symbols of a simpler day, a quieter time in our history that lots of us reach back for from time to time. For many of us, the old iron stove in the parlor is a comforting link with the past. Our stove may arrive in the bed of a brand-new, green pick-up truck instead of a horse-drawn wagon, but with it will come the same friendly warmth that it brought our ancestors generations ago.

It's kind of heartwarming to think about, isn't it?

Jacquelyn Peake

Thanksgiving Thoughts

He ripens fields of golden grain,
Greens the lawns with summer's rain,
Sets the fruit on plant and vine,
Adorns roadsides with columbine.

He gives the birds a song to sing,
Provides the wind for kites on string;
He sets the sun when evening's here
And watches o'er us all the year.

In autumn when the crops and hay
Are harvested and stored away,
I'm sure He'll find the time to spare
To listen to a thankful prayer.

Faye M. Estabrooks

Thank You, Father

In humbleness, we thank You, Father,
For the goodness You have shown,
For the blessings and compassion,
For comfort when we walk alone.

Thank You for our daily bounty,
For the love we share each day.
Thank You for the right to worship,
Each in our own chosen way.

Thank You for your hand that guides us,
Right from wrong, in all we do.
May we grow in understanding,
Always grateful — thanking You.

Bill Carr

Like No Other Time of the Year

Thanksgiving time is like no other time of the year. It's an invigorating time just before winter's chill, a time of expectation. It is the twilight of the seasons, one of nature's mysterious moods. The golden glow of autumn turns to muted shades of brown, as the leaves of pin oaks refuse to sever ties with their source of strength. They wither on their branches, clinging tenaciously, while their neighbors add to the groundswell. The sky is gray with a promise of snow, but it's not quite ready; it must tease us first. We feel a childish excitement knowing that at any moment, we may leap into winter completely at the mercy of something far more enduring than we are.

There is a strange and powerful beauty in the season's afterglow. After the waning of summer and the gilding of autumn, serene November, with its stillness and its scent of impending winter, invites us into the woods. Then, with equal pleasure, it invites us back indoors to the hearth where a firelight's warmth will welcome us.

Coming home is part of November's twilight mood. What better time for a Thanksgiving feast! With hearts warmed by the season, our sense of gratefulness is restored. We are thankful for family, for friends, for God's world. The mood lingers. Appetites dwell on things long-remembered. The golden bird brings with it the memory of Thanksgivings long past and the anticipation of more to come. Strange that we should be touched by so simple a thing as a meal. But it is much, much more than a meal. It's like no other time of the year.

Beth K. Wallach

The Twilight of Thanksgiving

The day has lengthened into eve,
And over all the meadows
The twilight's silent shuttles weave
Their sombre web of shadows;
With northern lights the cloudless skies
Are faintly phosphorescent,
And just above yon wooded rise
The new moon shows her crescent.

Before the evening lamps are lit,
While day and night commingle,
The sire and matron come and sit
Beside the cozy ingle;
And softly speak of the delight
Within their bosoms swelling,
Because beneath their roof tonight
Their dear ones all are dwelling.

And when around the cheerful blaze
The young folks take their places,
What blissful dreams of other days
Light up their aged faces!
The past returns with all its joys,
And they again are living
The years in which, as girls and boys,
Their children kept Thanksgiving.

William D. Kelly

Painting Opposite
by George Hinke

Quiet Time

All the leaves have fallen;
The sky is dark and gray.
There's a chilly wind a-blowing;
Winter's on the way.

Twilight comes so early,
And folks all hurry home
For some cozy warmth and comfort;
They're content now not to roam.

Lamplights cast a golden glow
To bring a bit of cheer.
You know, I'm kind of glad
The quiet time is here.

It gives us all a chance to sit
At home and rest awhile;
To draw closer to our families,
To talk, to laugh, to smile.

LaVerne P. Larson

Sweet Repose

When lacework of the leafless trees
Is etched on graying skies,
And, with swiftly moving clouds,
November winds arise,

Nature falls asleep. Another
Year comes to a close.
The solemn side of nature reigns
And rules o'er sweet repose.

In the hush of autumn,
The earth lies bare and still,
The grass is dry and rusty
On the distant hills,

But beyond the barren meadows,
In calm serenity,
Pine trees, tall and living,
Proclaim eternity.

Anna M. Reynolds

Final Season

The sullen calm of a threatening sky,
The lonely sound of a wild bird's cry;
A hushed world as snowflakes start...
Winter patterns in the heart.

Ernestine Lamont

Meditation

I wandered by the river's edge
As daytime fell asleep,
And watched the sunset through the trees
Sink in the forest deep.

I listened to the river's song,
'Twas like a lullaby,
Singing, soothing, it rambled on
Reflecting the evening sky.

Gertrude Rudberg

Down to Sleep

November woods are bare and still;
November days are clear and bright;
Each noon burns up the morning's chill;
The morning's snow is gone by night.
Each day my steps grow slow, grow light,
As through the woods I reverent creep,
Watching all things lie down to sleep.

I never knew before what beds,
Fragrant to smell, and soft to touch,
The forest sifts and shapes and spreads;
I never knew before how much
Of human sound there is in such
Low tones as through the forest sweep,
When all wild things lie down to sleep.

Helen Hunt Jackson

Earthbound

One morning, against a crystal sky,
I watched the flight of a swan.
A graceful, white-winged line he flew
At the edge of a rose-gold dawn.

He'd flown a path no compass knew
From the shores of some far-flung sea.
His lonely far-skied haunting call
Seemed a message just for me.

"Come, follow me," he seemed to say,
"Where the north wind never blows.
Come, follow me to a distant land
That only the wild swan knows."

Earthbound, I stood in that rose-gold dawn
Steadfast in the frozen snow,
But I wished for wings that could carry me
To the place where the wild swans go.

Mike Logan

Now Thank We All Our God

Martin Rinkart
Trans. by Catherine Winkworth

Johann Crüger

1. Now thank we all our God With heart and hands and voic - es,
2. O may this boun-teous God Through all our life be near us,
3. All praise and thanks to God The Fa - ther now be giv - en,

Who won-drous things hath done, In whom His world re - joic - es;
With ev - er joy - ful hearts And bless - ed peace to cheer us;
The Son, and Him who reigns With them in high - est heav - en,

Who, from our moth - er's arms, Hath blessed us on our way
And keep us in His grace And guide us when per - plexed,
The one e - ter - nal God Whom earth and heav'n a - dore;

With count - less gifts of love, And still is ours to - day.
And free us from all ills In this world and the next.
For thus it was, is now, And shall be ev - er - more.

Photo Opposite
CONGREGATIONAL CHURCH
Fryeburg, ME
Dick Smith

Jack Frost

With Winter comes a lively pace,
Frost bewhiskers Nature's face,
Chimney smoke rings melt the air,
And snowmen join the human race.

At fireside, friends seek to share
The warmth and glow of moments rare,
And children peer through crusty lace
At evergreens with angels' hair.

Leonore Huckleberry

Sure Signs

Someone painted pictures on my
Windowpane last night —
Willow trees with trailing boughs
And flowers, frosty white,

And lovely crystal butterflies;
But when the morning sun
Touched them with its golden beams,
They vanished one by one!

Helen Bayley Davis

Ideals Brings Christmas Cheer

Enjoy the sights and sounds of the holiday season in Christmas Ideals, our next issue.

Sparkling snow scenes and warm images of holiday joy and hospitality are part of a dazzling display of color photography that accompanies our selection of Christmas poems and stories.

A special presentation of the first Christmas features the religious art of Robert A. Heuel and inspiring passages from Handel's "Messiah."

Join us in the happiest celebration of the year and share the joy. Put Ideals' subscriptions at the top of your Christmas shopping list; they're the perfect gifts for friends and loved ones.

As one reader tells us, "I've given so many copies of Ideals away as gifts... I wonder if you realize how many lives it reaches and touches!" (A. A., Philadelphia, Pennsylvania)

ACKNOWLEDGMENTS

JACK FROST by Helen Bayley Davis originally published in *The Christian Science Monitor*, 1929; ALL IN A WORD by Aileen Fisher originally published in *Jack and Jill*, 1955, reprinted by permission of the author; FRANKLIN'S CHOICE from THE WRITINGS OF BENJAMIN FRANKLIN, edited, with introduction, by Albert Henry Smyth (New York: Macmillan, 1905-1907); THE DAY THE GEESE LANDED by Iris Hanson originally published in *Farm Wife News*, Box 643, Milwaukee, WI 53201; SONG OF THANKSGIVING from FORGOTTEN RAPTURE by Edna Greene Hines; SQUANTO PLANTS THE CORN by Gloria Maxson originally published in *Arizona Highways*, 1969; SOME SMALL GIFT and THANKSGIVING from HEART LEAVES, copyright 1954 by Mamie Ozburn Odum, Banner Press Publishers; WARMING THE HEART OF AMERICA by Jacquelyn Peake from COUNTRY SCENE, Volume 2, Number 4, copyright © 1977 by Ideals Publishing Corporation; THANKSGIVING DAY from FOR DAYS AND DAYS by Annette Wynne, copyright 1919 by Frederick A. Stokes Company; PSALM 92: 1-4 from REVISED STANDARD VERSION OF THE BIBLE, copyrighted 1946, 1952, © 1971, 1973. Our sincere thanks to the following authors whose addresses we were unable to locate: Carl Goeller for THE LEGEND OF THE CHRYSANTHEMUM; Helen D. Hering for AUTUMN GLORY from RIB MOUNTAIN ECHOES; Leonore Huckleberry for SURE SIGNS; Kate J. Rust for AUTUMN BONFIRES by Hazel Adell Jackson; and Anna M. Reynolds for SWEET REPOSE.